F...
Planes

Ian Rohr

Blake
EDUCATION

Lexile® measure: 560L
For more information visit: www.Lexile.com

Brainwaves Blue
Fighter Planes
ISBN 978 1 86509 922 4

Blake Education Pty Ltd
ABN 50 074 266 023
Locked Bag 2022
Glebe NSW 2037
Ph: (02) 8585 4085
Fax: (02) 8585 4058
Email: info@blake.com.au
Website: www.blake.com.au

Series publisher: Katy Pike
Series editors: Sophia Oravecz and Garda Turner
Designers: Matt Lin and Cliff Watt
Illustrators: Matt Lin and Aaron Lin

Picture credits: Images on pages 6, 7 (top), 14-18,
19 (bottom), 20, 21 (top), 24-27 supplied courtesy
of US Air Force. Image on page 7 (bottom)
supplied courtesy of US Department of Defense.
Image on page 19 (top) supplied courtesy of the
US Army.

Printed by Green Giant Press

CONTENTS

Faster Than Sound

You shoot into the sky, 5 kilometres in 10 seconds, spin around and dive straight down. Now, with a BOOM, you're flying faster than sound.

This is a fighter plane. Climb into the cockpit and grab the controls.

Fast Flyers

Modern, fighter planes are high-speed machines. They need to be. **Pilots** are flying to places where they are not welcome. The enemy will have their own planes and deadly weapons.

How a jet engine works

Jet engines burn a mixture of fuel and air. This makes hot gases, which give thrust. Thrust gets a plane off the ground and keeps it moving.

Ready for take off!

Turn that thing off!

Planes get their speed from powerful jet engines.

Off to get milk for coffee!

Many fighter planes are light to help them turn and move.

Fighter planes must also be **agile**. They fly into narrow valleys and skim low over mountains. They need to dodge their way out of trouble and attack at the same time.

Yikes! Hot engine!

7

Double Trouble

The F/A-18 Hornet is a classic fighter. It can twist and turn like a snake in the sky. It can fly in low to hit a target and then speed away.

F/A-18 Hornet breaks the sound barrier – flying at more than 1 200 kilometres per hour.

Q: What is red and black and buzzes at 11 000 metres in the air?

A: *A ladybird in an aeroplane.*

Weeeee!

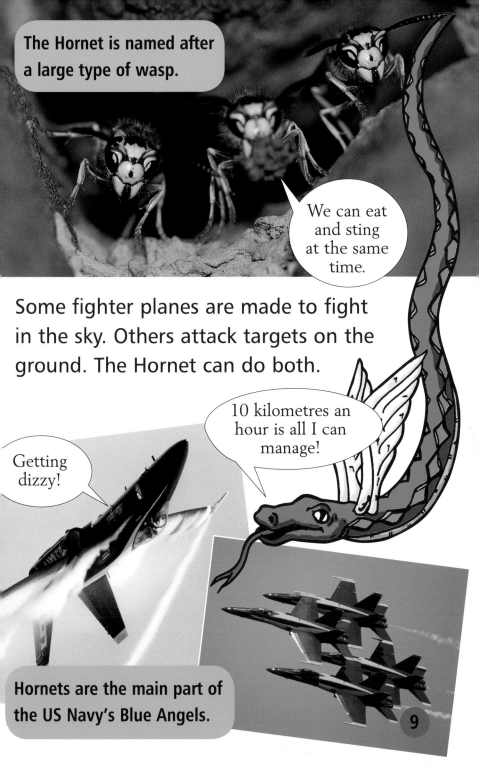

The Hornet is named after a large type of wasp.

We can eat and sting at the same time.

Some fighter planes are made to fight in the sky. Others attack targets on the ground. The Hornet can do both.

10 kilometres an hour is all I can manage!

Getting dizzy!

Hornets are the main part of the US Navy's Blue Angels.

9

Jets and Pieces

Where does this piece go?

No other fighter can be **modified** like the Hornet. Parts are added to it so that it can fight in different ways. The Hornet can be a high-flying fighter. It can also attack ground targets.

I'd rather fly the V Formation.

F/A-18C Hornets fly in Echelon Formation.

The Hornet can carry over 20 kinds of missiles. And it can defend itself. It has a six-barrel cannon in its nose. The cannon can shoot 6 000 rounds a minute!

The F/A-18C Hornet with missiles. "F" stands for Fighter.

What does the A stand for?

Plane	Pilots	Wingspan	Speed	Cost
B-2	2	52.12 metres	faster than sound	US$2 billion
F-14	2	19.54 metres	faster than sound	US$38 million
F/A-18	1-2	11.43 metres	faster than sound	US$39.5 million
F-117A	1	13.2 metres	faster than sound	US$45 million
KC-10	4	50 metres	1 000 km/h	US$88.4 million

It's Out There Somewhere ...

It twists and turns like a giant, black boomerang.

It's huge, but when it flies it's almost invisible. This is not something from a sci-fi movie. This is the **stealth** bomber – the B-2.

Nothing on the radar ...

Speedy and Stealthy

The B-2 is massive. At 52 metres across, it is wider than an Olympic swimming pool. But to enemy **radar** it's the size of a tiny bird.

Has to be sneaky ...

Why was the stealth bomber invented?

America wanted a long-range bomber and a plane that could fly over countries without being seen. The B-2 did both.

Weirdest bat I've ever seen!

From the back, the B-2's flat shape makes it hard to spot.

He he he, can't see me!

The B-2 Spirit is better known as the stealth bomber. "B" stands for Bomber.

To be invisible, a plane must be hard to see. It must also be quiet. And most importantly, radar must not be able to find it. So how does the giant stealth bomber hide?

HUH?

Passenger: These engines are too noisy.
Pilot: OK, I'll turn them off.

What?

Silent Spirit

Boo!

The B-2's 'flying wing' shape tricks any radar that comes looking for it. The outside of the plane also has a special coating. The radar waves bounce off in all directions.

The B-2 has no sharp edges or angles. It is all curves.

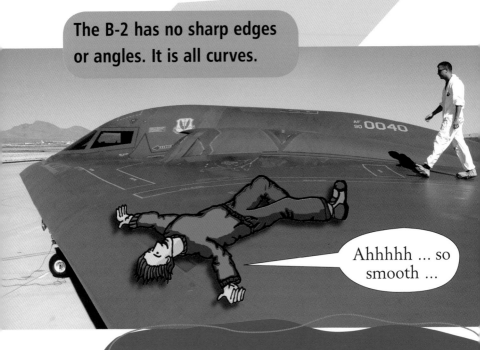

Ahhhhh ... so smooth ...

What is a flying wing?
Most planes have wings and a body. The B-2 is one, giant wing. This means the whole of its shape is helping it to fly.

The engines are inside the plane, to keep them quiet. And the B-2 has a low, flat shape. This makes it hard to see at night. Even in the day it is hard to see which way it's going.

I'm flying backwards, what about you?

The stealth bomber has few exhaust fumes, making it hard to spot.

The flying frypan and shoe

Is It Worth It?

2 billion dollars!

This big plane might look like a visitor from the future but it's real. It's great, but the B-2 isn't perfect. It's expensive to make and to maintain.

No wonder the B-2 tricks radar!

At a cost of around two billion dollars per plane, the B-2 is not cheap. It also needs **maintenance** to keep it going. This costs a lot and takes time.

A helicopter that hides

The RAH-66 Comanche is the world's first stealth helicopter. Its edges and coating deflect radar. Plus, its engines are very quiet.

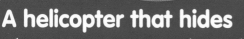

You sure this is on? I can't hear a thing.

exhaust nozzles

in-flight refuelling receptacle

engine intake

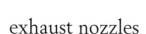

turbofan engines

two-person cockpit

fuel tanks (in wings)

bomb bay (middle of plane, behind cockpit)

A Hidden Hawk

Now, there are other stealth aircraft. The F-117A Nighthawk can also avoid radar and hide from the enemy. The Nighthawk is great at flying into hard-to-get-at places. It can hit small, well-protected, **strategic** targets.

The drag chute slows down the F-117 Nighthawk when it lands.

20

The US Air Force has about 60 Nighthawks.

These single-seat planes flew more than 1 200 missions in the 1991 Gulf War. Not one Nighthawk was hit by the enemy.

Trouble Strikes!

At top speed, your fighter plane is in trouble.

You've run out of fuel and you need to land. But there's no runway!

Fighter planes are made to save your skin. Let's look for an escape plan.

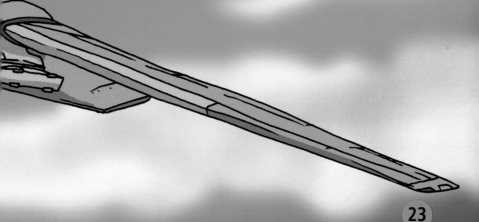

Mile High Petrol Stations

It's not good to run out of fuel 10 000 metres up. This is where a **refueller** plane can help. The refueller can refill a fighter plane in midair flight.

Night lights make the KC-10 a 24-hour station.

Fill 'er up and clean the windows.

Me Autopilot.

Q: How many pilots does it take to change a light bulb?

A: None. That's a job for the autopilot.

Hi, Captain John.

inside the cockpit of a KC-10A Extender

Cough! I just swallowed a fly!

The KC-10 Extender can carry 160 000 kilograms of fuel. A hose line is used to move the fuel to the other aircraft. KC-10s can fill up all kinds of military aircraft.

KC-10s can also carry up to 75 people and over 75 000 kilograms of cargo.

Ooooo, that's a lot of stuff!

Eject, Eject!

Pilots only pull the ejector handle when there is no other way out. This is the 'eject or die' decision. After a pilot pulls the handle – **BANG**! In four seconds it's all over.

Most of the time, all parts of the system work. And fast. About 9 out of 10 pilots survive the short, sharp shock of a high-speed ejection.

Pilots can be hurt by the extreme force of an ejection.

Oww! I hit my head!

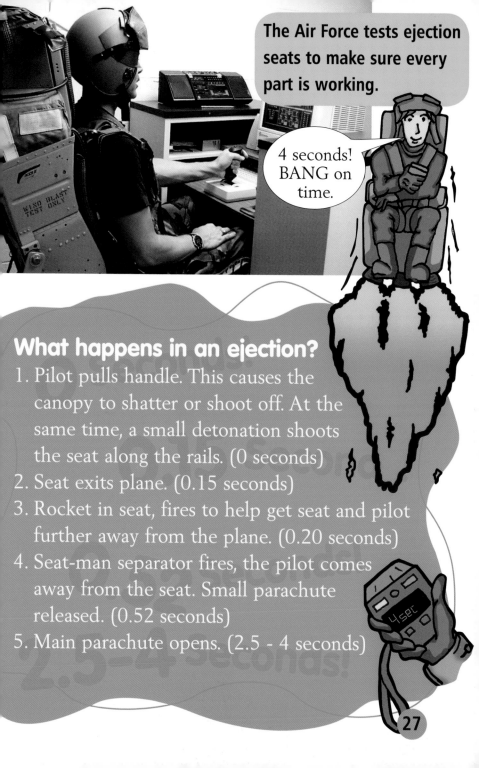

The Air Force tests ejection seats to make sure every part is working.

4 seconds! BANG on time.

What happens in an ejection?

1. Pilot pulls handle. This causes the canopy to shatter or shoot off. At the same time, a small detonation shoots the seat along the rails. (0 seconds)
2. Seat exits plane. (0.15 seconds)
3. Rocket in seat, fires to help get seat and pilot further away from the plane. (0.20 seconds)
4. Seat-man separator fires, the pilot comes away from the seat. Small parachute released. (0.52 seconds)
5. Main parachute opens. (2.5 - 4 seconds)

Swing Wings and Jumping Jets

I'm Super Wing!

Wide wings help get a plane off the ground. They also slow it down in the sky. Swing wings solve this problem. On fighters like the F-14 Tomcat, the wings sweep back once the jet is in the air.

Tomcat ready, meow!

The pilot and radar intercept officer enter the F-14A Tomcat.

The Harrier is a well-known type of jump-jet.

During a war it can be hard to find a runway. Some planes can take off and land on the one spot. Jump-jets can push up from the ground.

Our jump-jet can also hop, skip and tap dance.

Fact File

The first bomb dropped on Berlin, Germany in World War II killed the zoo's only elephant.

World War I fighter pilots, sitting in open cockpits, sometimes shot at each other with pistols.

Missed me!

Unpiloted Combat Air Vehicles (UCAVs) are being developed. These are basically robot aircraft that can be used as reusable missiles.

R4D7

Glossary

agile   able to move and turn quickly

maintenance taking care of something to keep it working well

modified changed to be used for something else

pilot   person who flies a plane

radar   a machine used to work out the presence and location of objects

refueller an aircraft that gives other planes fuel in midair

stealth   secret and hidden

strategic in war, targets that are very important to find and destroy

Index